HABITS OF SUCCESSFUL CAREER NOMADS

BY: NIKITA GUPTA, MBA

COPYRIGHT 2016

HTTP://WWW.HABITSOFSUCCESSFULCAREERNOMADS.COM

TABLE OF CONTENTS

"Keep your eyes on the stars, and your feet on the ground." Theodore Roosevelt

INTRODUCTION

Do you daily question, when will I be promoted? Should I stay with my current employer?

Have you ever wondered what if I left to find another job so that I could get that well deserved and earned promotion along with all the much needed financial benefits?

We did! Weary of waiting for our next job promotions and endless promises going unfulfilled we took action to grow in our careers on our own terms. And what were/are the results? Not only financial success, business success, but more!

Hence this book has been written by my husband and I as a means for new graduates and seasoned business professionals alike to create the ultimate career journey for yourself. Collectively, we have over a quarter of a century of sales, business development, product management, and marketing experience and have proven techniques that can help you go to the next level in your career today. That is if you are ready?

TAKING A LEAP

In 2008, when my husband and I got married we had grandiose plans of moving to Houston, TX to start our new life together. My husband had become infatuated with watching the HGTV show, Flip this House with Armando Montelongo. So much so that I think in the back of his mind he thought he could be Armando Montelongo.

However, what he really craved in watching the show based out of Houston, TX was more. More than just the Midwestern dream of being born in a city, getting a job there, raising a family there, and then seeing out your last days there. I know this works out perfectly fine for many of us, but it didn't work out for us. Instead we found ourselves becoming nomads for the sake of our careers, seeing the world, making new friends, building connections, and living a fuller life than we planned or anticipated.

FROM MIDWESTERNS TO SOUTHERNS

When we left Illinois and Michigan for Houston, TX we imagined a new life together with:

- An uncharacteristically lower cost of living.

- Better weather (no snow, slush, or ice).

- No state income tax.

- Diversity galore, thanks to HGTV's, Flip This House.

I had left my energy sales job with JCI as an Account Executive in MI. I was eager to grow in my career and help Carrier Corporation start a new energy services division as a Business Development Manager. My husband had left his job as a Midwest Director of Sales based out of MI &IL. Things were financially rocky for us at first. Due to a mounting of unplanned expenses we gathered in the midst of a hurricane, we ended up with <u>only $11</u> in our checking account. Our savings account was previously exhausted because we had just got married and returned from our honeymoon. Additionally, my husband had left his Director of Sales job without securing a new job ahead of our arrival to Texas.

However, within two weeks he was presented with his first job offer. He wasn't passionate about taking the job and so he continued to interview and six weeks later he landed his dream job as a Director of Business Development. With his new job in place and our finances having time to rebound we immersed ourselves into everything Texas. My husband was so enthusiastic about living in Texas that he brought his first cowboy hat and teased about getting boots with spurs. Six months later, I delightfully landed my first multi-million dollar deal and was inducted into a program to become a V.P. in 5 years. That was until I found out that Carrier purchased an energy services company and my father-in- law was going to need triple bypass heart surgery. Looking back on that time we laugh now, but the challenge to balance a new marriage, joint finances, and broader family strife was a serious strain that allowed us to see the foundation our marriage was built on.

FROM THE MIDWEST TO THE SOUTHEAST

My husband flew from Texas to Michigan several times over the course of a few weeks to be by his father's side as he underwent surgery and recovery. It was then that he felt an ever growing deep tug for us to move back to Michigan to be with his extended family; especially to look after his Mom. Fortunately, Carrier was understanding and allowed me to transfer to Michigan to open an office for their new energy services arm and my husband decided to go into business for himself. It was timely that we didn't end up purchasing a home in Texas that we would have had to rent out or sale; we can thank the financial crisis for that.

Living in Michigan raised a new set of challenges for us. We moved back into the home we had purchased in MI prior to our wedding. Due to the economic downturn in 2008 we did not sell the home but leased it out. Now back in our possession we had a permanent living solution, or so we thought. We were finally back, and within a short drives reach of my husband's family. We had not given any thought to how during the first 18 months of our marriage we were free. Free to figure out our struggles, to travel, to go out, and to focus on all things us. We didn't think about how transitioning back to Michigan brought with it substantial expectations: to attend my husband's niece's and nephew's gymnastics meets and soccer matches each week, to have family breakfast and/or dinner several times a week, and to attend any and all Indian functions.

Even though, my husband and I didn't travel for work, we realized that we didn't have the "time" together we once had because of all the obligations. It just seemed like our freedom/our island had been taken from us. And of course we couldn't say no to family and friends. Some months later we realized that we needed a new start/adventure. We had no idea that beginning down the path of a new start, again, would lead us to becoming career nomads; "true mercenaries" for the highest paying employer. Seemingly, the decision we made to move was now about us focusing on each other. However, little did we realize how this move would set-up our career trajectory and help us move closer to our ever evolving life goals.

Now in 2010, we knew that our next move would be crucial. We had amassed three properties in Michigan. The US economy was still trying to recuperate from the financial crisis of 2008 and the collapse of the auto industry so we had to figure out what to do with each home. We made the choice to continue leasing out each of our condos, condos we had individually owned prior to marriage. Our only dilemma was our marital house. Financially speaking, we couldn't move again and create a new start by carrying the burden of the house as well. We didn't want to lease it out because the rental income would no longer cover the entire mortgage. Hence we sought career opportunities where relocation was provided.

Within 3 months of making this decision, my husband found himself being recruited by two large multinational companies for his non replicable talents. One offer came with no relocation package but a large enough signing bonus for us to manage things. However we had to move to Washington, DC. His second offer included a relocation package that would cover the loss on sale of our house but was for less money. This job was in Raleigh, NC. Both offers were a blessing during challenging economic circumstances and we are grateful that we even had opportunities.

As a result, we ended up spending countless nights debating the pros and cons of both offers. Having moved previously to Houston and then back to Michigan, we were keen to make a wise choice. We knew that eventually we wanted to start a family and have stability so we dueled around the pluses and minuses of: quality of life, cost of living, education, and more importantly where I could quickly land a job, so we didn't end up in the same financial distress we had earlier in our marriage.

Ultimately, we decided on Raleigh, NC because I had travelled there some months prior for work and had fallen in love with its quaint southern charm. So we sold our martial home in Michigan and moved to Raleigh, NC. I ended up finding a new job ahead of our relocation to North Carolina, as a Director of Sales & Business Development and we started to make friends.

The company I worked for was headquartered in Charlotte, NC and my husband saw his travel schedule pick up. He would always travel from Raleigh, NC to Charlotte, NC and then to his destination. All of this combined with the fact that we couldn't find a house we loved in Raleigh, NC propelled us to move to Charlotte, NC. We would be in Charlotte, NC for the next 3 years until I became pregnant and the company I worked for now as a Vice President of Sales, Marketing, and Business Development no longer fit into our life plan. Or at least my pregnancy didn't fit into their plans. I couldn't believe I was fired for being pregnant.

FIRED FOR BEING PREGNANT!

Pure Hell! During my 5th month of pregnancy, I was fired from my job as a Vice President of Sales, Marketing, and Business Development for a start-up company. The laws in the U.S. did not protect me as an expectant mother because the company I worked for had less than 15 employees. Of course, I was traumatized with 7 months under my belt, thousands of frequent flyer miles racked up, a sales territory spanning 8 states, and a baby coming soon. My sales pipeline was active, robust, and I was progressing thru the sales process; clasping approximately $30 Million in sales opportunities that I had built from the ground up.

It was an eerie afternoon phone call in which neither owner could justify their termination of my employment. They merely stated that things weren't going to work out. In the back of my mind, I had recalled telling one of the owners that I was expecting two weeks prior to this phone call and his reply showed me it was not well received. He stated "You're going to gain 30lbs; what are you going to do; how are you going to do your job?" In shock, I replied I'm still going to do my job, be and look professional, and bring in the deals I'm working on. Once home I expressed my anxiety about the matter to my husband. He attempted to reassure me that there was no way they would/could let me go because I was pregnant. Could they?

After the phone call took place, I sobbed and bemoaned the situation the entire weekend. However when Monday arrived I took action and with these actions I landed a job offer 6 weeks later. Considering that I was now 6.5 months pregnant I decided not to take the job and focus on my pregnancy, but it was a moral victory. After the baby had arrived we again began to rethink our life plan and perhaps it being best that we were closer to family. As a result, we pondered yet another move. This move wasn't in the plans when we moved down to North Carolina, as we thought first Raleigh, NC then Charlotte, NC would be our home for some time to come. Again the notion of stability, even more so now with a baby played a significant part in our decision.

A LEAP TO THE CENTRAL, US AND BACK

Seeing and having this new baby girl, this new life in our care propelled us to take our next leap. We knew we didn't want to reside in IL or MI since we had previously left MI to focus on our marriage. When I got the call about a multinational company looking for a sales leader in Missouri my husband and I said to ourselves that it. Moving to Missouri presented the opportunity for both of us to see our families more.

I received an offer to relocate to St. Louis, MO, two months after having our daughter to spear head energy sales for a multinational company. My husband explained the situation to his boss who stated that he was open to him living anywhere in the US as long as there was an airport. Thus we were once again excited for a new start/adventure with our daughter in tow.

Our daughter was a trooper. She logged approximately 30,000 miles in her car seat during her first year of life as we attempted to get acclimated to St. Louis. We knew St. Louis had a bad rap but also that it was a city ripe for growth. Additionally, my mom was eager to be our daughter's caretaker while I worked. She had indicated through several conversations that she would happily drive down from Illinois every week. This was a conversation we vetted several times prior to making the decision to move there.

However this is not how things panned out. My mom could only be available to help on occasion and so my husband and I had to balance our work schedules from home to take care of our daughter. Additionally we weren't prepared for the breadth of racial tension and crime that fused into a tornado after Michael Brown was killed. The race riots were going on just 5 miles from the condo we rented. My husband some days later was pulled over for no reason while driving on Lindbergh Dr. and then prior to our departure from St. Louis he was accused of robbing the condo we rented in broad daylight. All of these factors lead us to be maladjusted to St. Louis and dread the environment we were raising our daughter in.

A year after I got my offer, we left St. Louis, MO and headed back to Charlotte, NC. My husband once again started a new work adventure as a Global Sales Director that was based on the East Coast and I had finally been greeted with an exit from Corporate America to start my own business and let you all know how we did it all.

"The first step to getting somewhere is to decide that you are not going to stay where you are." UNKNOWN

WHAT IS A NOMAD?

Conventionally when you hear the word nomad you imagine someone wandering to and fro across the earth. This particular person doesn't have a place to go; if they do it is a temporary location and not a real "home". With ease this person moves or relocates from one location to another. They are often driven by the need to: put food on the table, find a job, being able to provide for their family, and being able to obtain/maintain a sense of financial security & well-being.

WHAT IS A CAREER NOMAD?

In our own words, a career nomad is a person that intentionally is readily available or open to relocating for their career. This person understands that the need to relocate will allow them the opportunity to grow in their career (climb the ever growing corporate ladder quicker) and gain financially.

BECOMING A CAREER NOMAD

Is not an easy feat but is also not hard. It is a decision to leave behind what you are accustomed to: family, friends, cities, etc., for the sake of financial gain and growth but it is doable. My husband and I ultimately became nomads for the sake of our careers. In the course of 7.5 years of marriage we have lived in 5 states and 8 cities. Being a career nomad has allowed us to: not only grow rapidly in our careers, but also provided for immediate career expansion, career visibility, an ability to travel more of the world, meet amazing people, live in new places, and garner novel experiences one city, plane, and car ride at a time.

HOW?

Put away the conventional thought that if you stay at your current job you are guaranteed a promotion with a new title etc. In today's economically uncertain times this may or may not be true. How can I say this? Well I had heard time and time again from my employers that I was next in line to become a Sales Manager, next in line to become a V.P.; I am on the "guaranteed" fast track to create a new arm for the company.

Yet the position would not be available for a while or until someone had retired. In essence, I would have to wait years to grow when I had already shown my dedication, exhausted my talent for the organization, and was more than qualified. Gone are the days of our parents generation, where working at a job for 30 years yielded pride, accomplishment, financial security, and wellbeing. We are part of the microwave generation, a generation that has access to information like no other generation before us. In this age, not being a career nomad put's many of us at a disadvantage when it comes to career growth in a competitive economic environment.

If you know you have the skills, passion, drive, and willingness to grow then you may just have to move to go to the next level or step in your career. The ultimate plan for any successful career nomad is to always seek growth while balancing every other personal situation. So in the pursuit of growth, how does one become a career nomad? Here are our 5 steps to becoming a career nomad.

5 STEPS TO BECOMING A CAREER NOMAD

1.) Determine if there is immediate career growth for you at your current organization. If there is, are you willing to wait? Also during this evaluation gauge if you are happy with your roles and responsibilities. Have you been able to have verifiable success at the current organization? If so, have you been compensated accordingly? Do you like the work environment? Is the company financially sound? Is there a documented growth plan for you? Are you in a growth segment where people of your skillset and talents are in high demand? Evaluation is very key and shouldn't be taken lightly as there are significant impacts to finances, family, and quality of life. If you are not willing to wait and are ready to grow then it's time to dust off your resume.

2.) Prior to posting or sending your resume to recruiters make sure that your resume is tailored to the job you want or are applying for, and appropriately showcases your talents, skillsets, accomplishments, and strengths. How? Research resumes online and in books that are in line with the ideal job that you are looking for and/or work with a resume company. This same tactic goes for your cover letter which is essential for submitting a resume to an online job posting. Research here is very important. A proper resume can either make you or break you as a candidate in the eyes of any company. Consider your resume to be a calling card, as most hiring managers and recruiters will briefly skim over or just quickly glance at your resume. It is imperative that your resume very clearly and quickly highlight you as a qualified candidate.

3.) Create and fine tune said resume and cover letter that is job appropriate. During this step, it is okay to ask people to review your resume. Remember that this is your calling card, more input and refinement help!

4.) Connect with recruiters and/or HR recruiters on career sites like LinkedIn, career builder, and the ladders. In particular, on LinkedIn this is easily done and you can even send an introduction email to find out about opportunities for growth in your field. What should the note/email to the company recruiter say? I will show you how and what to say in the next step. It is so simple, but most people don't take the time or make the effort. Here goes.

Sample of a LinkedIn introduction email to a company recruiter.

Often time's recruiters and/or HR recruiters have open positions that they are hiring for and post this information online. Conduct a job search for a position that is of interest to you on LinkedIn. Once you find this job posting look at who the company recruiter is on LinkedIn. After you find this information, contact this person via LinkedIn with a short message.

Example

Hi, my name is John Doe and I have been in sales for the past 10 years. I am interested in networking with you on LinkedIn.

There is no reason for the recruiter to not connect with you if you are in the industry they are in and also if your LinkedIn profile showcases your accomplishments.

What kind of accomplishments?

Skill endorsements and recommendations from your current and former colleagues, peers, bosses, customers and others aware of your successes should be on display. Once connected you can thank them for linking in with you and mention that you saw a posting/advertisement for the job you are interested in and wanted to find out if the opportunity was still available.

Again, recruiters are looking to find the best candidates for the companies they work for and they will be more than willing to give you more input on this opportunity and even connect you to the hiring manager based on your inquiry.

As I mentioned before, we are part of the microwave generation, with access to an infinite array of information. Use the information and technology to your benefit.

5.) Submit your resume and cover letter to organizations that are of interest to you directly or via LinkedIn, salesjobs.com, monster, simply hired, indeed, career builder, the ladders etc. and of course go interview!

*** *Make sure that you have a top 5 list of places that you are willing to move to. Recruiters are sure to ask you these questions.*

Are you willing to relocate?

If so where?

If you want to stay closer to where your family is make sure you have geographically looked at the options for the jobs the recruiter has or those you've found online and have applied to.

CAREER NOMAD GET THE JOB

BUILDING A RESUME SUITED TO FINDING YOUR NEXT JOB!

Prior to posting or sending your resume to recruiters and/or HR Managers make sure that your resume and cover letter are tailored to the job you want or are applying for. You need to make sure these two documents appropriately show cases your talents, skillsets, accomplishments, and strengths.

How?

Research resumes online and in books that are in line with the ideal job that you are looking for and/or work with a resume company. This same tactic goes for your cover letter which is essential for submitting a resume to an online job posting. Research here is very important. A proper resume can either make you or break you as a candidate in the eyes of any company. Consider your resume to be a calling card, as most hiring managers and recruiters will briefly skim over or just quickly glance at your resume. It is imperative that your resume very clearly and quickly highlights you as a qualified candidate.

Below are some resume MUSTS!

Length   Your resume should be 1 page, 2 pages max. It should be brief and to the point!

Margins   1" all sides

Font   Use one of the Times fonts (i.e. Times New Roman, CG Times or Times)

Font size   The size of the font should be no smaller than 9 and no larger than 16

Dates   All dates should be in reverse chronological order within any section.

Do not include the months. Instead use years and/or seasons.

For example: 2011-2012

2011-Present

Sections **EDUCATION** must be the first subject. **EXPERIENCE** must be the second subject.

Never include a picture, marital status, or age

Do not use the words "I", "me", or "my" in your resume.

Putting Your Resume Together Soundly

Name & Address

At the top of your resume should be the following: Name at left margin or centered on first line of resume.

Use All CAPS, Bold, 20 or 18 font size.

Your name should be the largest font on your resume.

Place a Horizontal Line underneath your name, before your address, and no space after the line.

Include your address, phone number and email directly after.

Font size should be 9-12 (no bigger than the font size of the body of the resume)

Use only one email address in your resume.

Example 1

JOHN DOE

Address: 2999 E. Livingston, VA 40009, 312-567-xxx, Email: johndoe@gmail.com

Example 2

JOHN DOE

Address: 2999 E. Livingston, VA 40009, 312-567-xxx, Email: johndoe@gmail.com

THE COVETED COVER LETTER

Drafting a cover letter suited to finding your next job. The coveted Cover letter is essential if you are applying directly to job postings online.

The cover letter has to be clear in its purpose IMMEDIATELY; you do not have the ability to clarify your message if it is not understood at the time its read. Make sure the cover letter directly answers 3 questions for the reader/its audience:

1.) Why are you writing to the company or organization?
2.) Why should the reader be interested in what you have to say?
3.) What actions are requested/will you take?

A cover letter should **_ALWAYS_** accompany your resume when the potential employer has indicated that you are to respond in writing.

Guidelines/TIPS

- It should be 1 page again brief and succinct. Save all the details/particulars for the interview.
- Always address the letter to a name, never a position. The first paragraph should indicate to who and why you are writing the letter. In the cover letter application mention how you knew there was an opening either an advertisement or a personal reference.
- The second paragraph should focus on your qualifications as they relate to the job you are seeking/applying for.
- Point out your skills and refer to your enclosed resume.
- The third paragraph should be action oriented asking for an appointment for a meeting or interview.
- Use 81/2x11 white or off-white bond paper. Print your resume and cover letter on the same type of paper.

- Write in your own words as if you are having a conversation.
- Be clear.
- Conclude the cover letter with a request for an interview, phone conversation etc.
- Avoid the constant use of I.
- Avoid the overuse of adjectives (loyal, devoted, dependable, hardworking)

REFERENCES

***You may be asked to provide professional references during your job search. This is traditionally a good sign that you are a final candidate for a position. You should contact and prepare a list of these references when you prepare your resume 3-4 should work. **Do not list the references on your resume.** Instead make sure to call your references and ask for their permission to use them as a reference. Update them on where you are at with your career planning, goals, job you are pursing. Call them after you hear the potential employer ask for your reference and let them know who you interviewed with, what position, and who will probably call them. Ask your reference to call you after the employer calls them.

- **Reference should include:**

- **Name and Relationship**

- **Title**

- **Organization Name**

- **Address**

- **Business Phone**

PREPARING FOR THE INTERVIEW & INTERVIEW QUESTIONS

The type of Interview you may end up partaking in depends on the organization. These are the most common types of job interviews:

- Telephone Interview (customarily takes place before a face-to-face interview)
- Sequenced interview
- Behavioral Interview

- Performance Interview
- Case Interview
- Meal Interview
- Testing

Preparing for the interview includes simple preparations such as:

- Knowing exactly where the interview will be held, what time, and how long it will take for you to arrive. You can practice your drive to and from your interview location in advance so you know how much time it will take you and plan for delays.

- Prepare, prepare, prepare! Listen to the recruiter, Human Resources Manager, and Hiring Manager about the job expectations. Ask questions and get answers. Do the same research for this job that you did to get your previous job. Research as mentioned is very important. It is amazing how many people don't actually prepare for an interview. Research the company, the financials, the growth perspectives, the products, the services, market activity, and consumer satisfaction.

- Understand the types of questions interviewers may ask you; look at online forum about the organization and questions they commonly ask during the interview process. Understanding and researching questions and then practicing answers helps create comfortability in the message you are trying to get across, while also making sure you are able to highlight all your strengths. Use technology to your advantage. A few extra hours of preparation can go a long way in differentiating yourself.

- Complete all application and employment forms.

- Bring several copies of your resume, a notepad to write things down and ask questions, and a writing instrument.

- Know the correct names and pronunciation of the individuals that will be interviewing you and vice versa (you are interviewing them to determine if it is a fit).

- Arrive a few minutes early and relax. Collect your thoughts, review your skills and abilities, and how you feel they apply to the organization.

- Be confident. Be the authority the job will expect you to be (the Manager, Sales Rep, VP, Director, Analyst, Nurse, Counselor etc). If you have researched the company and the roles and responsibilities correctly this should be easy. Again, you are talking about your successes here so be confident.

- Know your strengths and let them shine. You are the industry expert. There is no better candidate for this job than you. Let every person you talk to see it and know it.

- Dress for the occasion/interview. Find a suit/business attire that makes you feel great when you wear it. It highlights your best features. Make sure you are well groomed.

The key here is to make sure you are dressed for success.

- Breathe. Getting the job may take numerous interviews depending on the opportunity you are going after. Envision the end but stay prepared and focused each and every step of the way. Don't forget to celebrate the milestones.

- Make sure that if you do have multiple interviews during the day that you take a snack with you that you can quickly eat in between interviews like a granola bar or banana. Eat breakfast or lunch depending on the time of day. The key here is to make sure you keep your energy level up. Interviewing is mentally exhausting.

- Get settled. If offered a cup of coffee, water, or a soft drink take it (you may end up needing it) Put it somewhere you will not bump or hit it.

During the Interview

Answer questions concisely. Do not ramble. Why?

1. It shows you listen.
2. It shows you quickly organize your thoughts.
3. It allows the interviewer to ask another pertinent questions (this takes practice).

Ask questions!

Don't say you don't have any questions when they ask you if you have questions. It makes the interviewer think you aren't interested and you weren't listening to them during the course of your interview. Ask 4-5 questions about the job. Leave benefits and salary questions until after you have received the offer.

SAMPLE QUESTIONS:

- Why did you decide to work for X company?

- How would you overcome X shortcomings?

- What would your 30, 60, 90 day plan be for me in this position?

- At the end of the interview find out what the next step is in the interviewing process. Thank the person and reiterate your excitement for the position and organization.

AFTER THE INTERVIEW

- Stay engaged. Particularly with the recruiter(s) you are working with and all persons you interviewed with. Continue to sell yourself and your capabilities until you have locked down/landed the job.

- After the interview make sure to send thank you emails to all the people that interviewed you. This is another good signal to employers that you actually follow-up. Even better, go buy a hallmark card and put a quick note in it to thank each person that interviewed you. It is an extra touch that is even more personable than email and that hardly anyone does. It will make you stand out.

OUR CAREER NOMAD SUCCESSES

Here are 7 Successes you too can realize by being or becoming a career nomad:

1. Owning numerous homes. It just comes with the territory of moving and relocating.   Sometimes it makes more financial sense to lease out a home rather than sell it.   It depends on your career growth and financial incentive gains, and there are risks, but the rewards give you another revenue stream.
2. Making a plenitude of new friends and lifelong connections.

3. The ultimate career growth! I've gone from Sales Executive to Business Development Director, to Vice President/Director of Sales to CEO of my own company. Every step of the way, I made sure to learn how I could pick up additional skillsets and have mentors that could provide me with great advice to lead me forward.

4. Better geographic conditions. No longer having to

deal with the harsh realities of horrible weather (i.e. snow, hail, earth quakes, hurricanes etc.)

5. Ability to travel and see the world.

6. Having a novel place for your family and friends to visit.

7. Ability to enjoy life more/live life to the fullest.

CAREER NOMAD LESSONS

Here are some life lessons us career nomads know all too well:

1.) The best luggage to travel with: Hard case suitcases.

2.) How to pack quickly. This is a skill you effortlessly learn overtime.

3.) The best companies to call for short and long-term storage: Short term-Pods, Long term-Corrigan.

4.) The best companies to call for moving locally and nationally: Two Men & a Truck & Corrigan.

5.) The best company for quick same day move it yourself: U-Haul.

6.) Renting vs buying new furniture. Rent if you don't know how long you are going to be in your new city for. Plan to grow. Best places for rental furniture CORT and Rent-A-Center. Also in most cases you can go to CORT and buy gently used furniture sets to deck out an entire apartment for the cost of just a few months of rent for new furniture.

7.) When moving, having someone else pack your house for you can be advantageous but not when it comes to your "truly personal" items.

8.) Be open to moving/relocating. Make sure it is a good fit for you and your family (if applicable), but do your research.

9.) Want career growth? Network, network, network! A great place to start is LinkedIn.

10.) Keep your resume updated and listen to your mentor/recruiter/HR on what to change as it relates to your resume this will help you stand out. Last know your job strengths and weaknesses and then work on both.

BONUS

Finding Friends in a new city can be stressful especially if you have kids. Here are 4 tips that we have utilized to make friends in each and every new city that we have lived in.

1) Be sociable and make friends with the people you meet at work.

2.) Leverage social media. Facebook is a great way to find "old" new friends from college or high school that are currently residing in your new city. Facebook is also great for meeting new parent friends as there are groups that are based in different cities. Feel free to visit the group page site at first and ease your way into this means of making new friends.

3.) Talk with and socialize with the neighbors in your new neighborhood/community. Join or volunteer for the HOA.

4.) Join running clubs, stroller clubs, walking clubs, mommy clubs, mommy and me groups, and fitness centers in your new city to make friends. Many of the clubs and groups mentioned can be found online.

FINAL THOUGHTS...WHAT NEXT?

Make a decision of where you want to be in your career. Envision it, write it down, recite it, and put it into action. Never be willing to settle for the status quo. Always seek growth and betterment. Your next job leap may just be a move away. Seize it!

ABOUT THE AUTHOR

NIKITA GUPTA, MBA IS A 16 YEAR SALES, BUSINESS DEVELOPMENT, AND MARKETING VETERAN. SHE AND HER HUSBAND HAVE OVER A QUARTER A CENTURY OF BUSINESS SUCCESSES. SHE STARTED OFF HER CAREER AS A SALES REP AND IS NOW RUNS HER OWN COMPANY. NIKITA AND HER HUSBAND ARE THE ULTIMATE CAREER NOMADS. SHE HAS BEEN IMPASSIONED TO HELP THOSE OF YOU THAT ARE INTERESTED IN SUCCESSFULLY CLIMBING THE CORPORATE JUNGLE WITHOUT A LADDER; UNDER YOUR OWN TERMS. SHE IS ALSO AN AUTHOR OF THE CHICAGO INITIATIVE.

FIND OUT MORE ABOUT HER AT:
HTTP://WWW.HABITSOFSUCCESSFULCAREERNOMADS.COM